P9-CKA-609

Designed by Flowerpot Press in Franklin, TN.
www.FlowerpotPress.com
Designer: Jonas Fearon Bell
Editor: Johannah Gilman Paiva
PAB-0808-0121
ISBN: 978-1-4867-0557-3
Made in China/Fabriqué en Chine

Why Do Tractors Have Such Big Tires?

Written by
Jennifer Shand

Illustrated by
Daniele Fabbri

Machines are cool!

Not only do they take us from place to place, but they also perform tasks we could never do on our own and make our lives much easier!

Why do TRACTORS have such BIG tires?

Is it so they can CRUSH
    the other MACHINES on the farm?

No, that's silly!

Tractors have big tires to help them
drive through tall grass, sticky
mud, or sometimes even
snow without getting stuck!

This is called having good traction.

Having big tires with good traction also makes tractors useful for pulling heavy equipment.

Why do some PLANES leave a long, white trail behind them when they ZOOM through the sky?

Is it because they are trying to make a PATH
to find their way back HOME?

No, that's silly!

A trail is made when a plane flies through air that is wet and cold, because the water from the plane's exhaust freezes in the cold air and makes a trail of ice.

Why do WASHING MACHINES spin and TUMBLE
the clothes round and round?

Is it because that is where the CLOTHES
go for GYMNASTICS class?

No, that's silly!

Washing machines spin and tumble clothes to get them as clean as possible!

The spinning and tumbling moves the clothes all around so they get wet and soapy all over. Moving the water and soap back and forth makes the soap powerful and sudsy!

After the water drains out, the machine spins really fast to shake as much water as it can from the clothes so they will dry faster.

Why do CRANES have such TALL towers?

Is it because they love to play BASKETBALL,
and especially love to DUNK?

No, that's silly!

Cranes have tall towers because they lift heavy things to high-up places! The tall tower is also called a "boom" or a "mast." Being very tall is very good, because it allows the crane to "leverage" the weight, or use a little bit of force on one end of the boom to lift something much heavier on the other end.

Why do TRAINS
have CONDUCTORS?

Is it because there is a
tiny, hidden ORCHESTRA
playing music for
all of the PASSENGERS?

No, that's silly!

A train conductor makes sure all the parts of a train work together to make a well-running train, just as an orchestra conductor helps all of the musicians work together to make beautiful music.

The conductor operates many controls, like the brakes and throttle, which control the train's speed, and has to manage the train's total weight, the route it will take, and make announcements to the passengers.

Machines are awesome!

There are thousands of
amazing machines at work
around us every day. Just think
of all the things we couldn't build
or do without them!

Machines have truly changed the
world and our lives!